A BEGINNER'S GUIDE TO
SUPER

ABUNDANCE

The New Economics of Time Prices

GALE L. POOLEY

Cover design by Faceout Studio.
Book design by Melina Yingling Enterline.
Photos: Getty Images.

Printed in the United States of America.

Paperback ISBN: 978-1-964524-50-4
eBook ISBN: 978-1-964524-51-1

Library of Congress Cataloging-in-Publication Data available.

Cato Institute
1000 Massachusetts Ave. NW
Washington, DC 20001
www.cato.org

CONTENTS

THANOS, EHRLICH, MALTHUS, AND SIMON

> The universe is finite, its resources finite.
> If life is left unchecked, life will cease to exist.
> It needs correcting.
>
> Thanos in *Avengers: Infinity War*

The Marvel supervillain Thanos is in search of superpowers that will allow him to destroy half the life in the universe. In his worldview, this is the moral thing to do. By reducing all life by half, he reasons, there will be plenty of resources left for the survivors. Where did Thanos get his ideas? His first appearance in a comic book was in 1973. Five years earlier, Stanford biologist Paul Ehrlich had published *The Population Bomb.* The book opens with this statement:

> The battle to feed all of humanity is over. In the 1970s hundreds of millions of people will starve to death in spite of any crash programs embarked upon now. At this late date nothing can prevent a substantial increase in the world death rate.

The book restates ideas published in 1798 by the English cleric Thomas Malthus. In *An Essay on the Principle of Population*, Malthus made the following argument:

> The power of population is indefinitely greater than the power in the earth to produce subsistence for man. Population, when unchecked, increases in a geometrical ratio. Subsistence increases only in an arithmetical ratio. A slight acquaintance with numbers will show the immensity of the first power in comparison of the second.

Ehrlich's *Population Bomb* sold millions of copies and made him famous. He appeared on television programs and was given numerous awards. Around that time, other similar books were published, including *Limits to Growth* and *A Blueprint for Survival*. Popular culture was also influenced by the first Earth Day on April 22, 1970, and movies such as *Soylent Green* and *Logan's Run*. The mood of the country was clearly pessimistic about the future.

Professor Julian Simon was then a young economics professor at the University of Illinois at Urbana-Champaign (in 1983, he moved to the University of Maryland, where he spent the rest of his career). After reading Ehrlich's book and reflecting on what he knew about economic incentives, Simon decided to check the historical prices of several nonrenewable resources, such as copper.

Prices are important because they contain information about the relative scarcity of goods—that is, products and services. If population is increasing and demand is increasing faster than supply, then prices should rise. To his surprise, Simon found that the long-term trend in prices had been declining—that as population has increased, prices have decreased. How was this possible? Simon theorized that as prices increase, people respond in four ways: consume less, search for more, look for substitutes, and recycle if possible. Those four factors will eventually lead to lower prices.

Simon published his findings in the journal *Science* in June 1980 in an article titled "Resources, Population, Environment: An Oversupply of False Bad News." He criticized Malthusian voices such as the National Wildlife Federation, the secretary-general of the United Nations, and Ehrlich. There was an immediate backlash from Ehrlich, and he and Simon began a heated public debate on the relationship between resources and population. At about that time, Simon challenged Ehrlich to a bet. "Offering to wager is the last recourse of the frustrated," Simon wrote. "When you are convinced that you have hold of an important idea, and you can't get the other side to listen, offering to bet is all that is

> Simon theorized that as prices increase, people respond in four ways: consume less, search for more, look for substitutes, and recycle if possible. Those four factors will eventually lead to lower prices.

left. If the other side refuses to bet, they implicitly acknowledge that they are less sure than they claim to be."

Ehrlich—who in 1970 went so far as to predict that "if I were a gambler, I would take even money that England will not exist in the year 2000"—and two of his friends from academia, John Holdren and John Harte, decided to "accept Simon's astonishing offer before other greedy people jump[ed] in." Ehrlich even quipped that "the lure of easy money can be irresistible," so Ehrlich's group bet $1,000 on $200 quantities of five metals: chrome, copper, nickel, tin, and tungsten. Then they signed a futures contract in September 1980 that stipulated that Simon would sell these same quantities of metal to Ehrlich's group for the same price in 10 years' time. If the inflation-adjusted prices increased, Simon would owe Ehrlich the difference. If the prices decreased, Ehrlich would owe Simon.

In October 1990, Ehrlich mailed Simon a check for $576.07. The prices of tin and tungsten had fallen by more than half. The inflation-adjusted prices had fallen by 36 percent. Ehrlich's wife, Anne, signed the check. There was no letter accompanying it.

As Simon had predicted, human ingenuity had made these resources more abundant despite a population increase of more than 870 million, the largest percentage increase in recorded history. New nickel mines had been discovered and exploited in Colombia, ending a Canadian monopoly on the commodity. Glass cables had replaced copper wires, driving down demand for the metal. Aluminum replaced tin in cans, eventually leading to the collapse of the price-setting international tin cartel. Across the board, technological improvement and entrepreneurship made mining and refining so much more efficient and therefore cheaper that new supply outpaced the rising demand of a growing population.

Superabundance, the 2022 book I coauthored with Marian Tupy that was inspired by the Simon–Ehrlich bet, asks two questions: (1) are we running out of resources, and (2) are there too many people? The book, using a new conceptual framework and a wide variety of examples, shows that resource abundance is increasing much faster than population growth. *Superabundance* introduces the new economics of knowledge, learning, and time (for more, see superabundance.com). This *Beginner's Guide to Superabundance* distills the book's findings in an easily accessible format. Wage data are for 2022 and some numbers have been rounded for consistency in presentation.

CHAPTER 1

MEASURING ABUNDANCE AT THE PERSONAL LEVEL

CHOCOLATE BARS

When I was a kid, my grandpa told me that when he was a kid, chocolate bars cost only $0.05. In 2022, a chocolate bar cost about $1.32 at my local Walmart. Although it is true that chocolate bars have gotten more expensive in absolute dollar terms, the real question is, "Have they become more or less affordable?" To answer this question, we have to compare the candy bar price with a person's hourly income. How much time did it take my grandpa to earn the money to buy his candy bar back in 1900 versus the time it takes today?

We buy things with money, but we pay for them with our time. It's really how much time it takes to earn the money to buy something that counts. So there are actually two prices: money prices and time prices. Money prices are expressed in dollars and cents, while time prices are expressed in hours and minutes. Converting a money price to a time price is simple. Divide the money price of a product or service by hourly income.

$$\text{Time Price } = \frac{\text{Money Price}}{\text{Hourly Income}}$$

As an unskilled worker in 1900, Grandpa earned about $0.09 per hour. That means the time price of his $0.05 chocolate treat was about 0.56 hours or 33 minutes. In 2022, unskilled wages were closer to $15.72 per hour. This wage would put the time price for unskilled workers at five minutes. For the time it took Grandpa to earn the money to buy one chocolate bar, in 2022 you could get more than six. You enjoy over 560 percent more chocolate abundance than Grandpa did. The following table provides the details on how we should use time to make our comparisons.

CHOCOLATE BARS

	1900	2022	Change	Percentage change
Price	$0.05	$1.32	$1.27	2,540%
Hourly compensation	$0.09	$15.72	$15.63	17,367%
Time price in hours	0.56	0.08	0.048	−86%
Time price in minutes	33	5	−28	−85%
Personal resource multiplier	1	7	6	600%

The personal resource multiplier is the start-year time price divided by the end-year time price. For the start year, the personal resource multiplier is always equal to 1. Note that as the time price decreases, personal resource abundance increases geometrically.

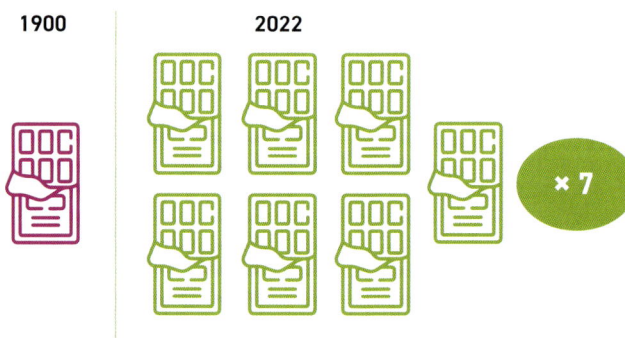

1900   2022

× 7

Let's look at some other products and services and see if they have become more or less abundant over time. Many more can be found in *Superabundance*.

SIX REASONS WHY TIME IS BETTER THAN MONEY TO MEASURE ABUNDANCE

Time is better than money to measure abundance, for six main reasons.

First, time prices contain more information than money prices. Looking only at prices, without also looking at wages, tells only half the story. Innovation lowers prices and increases wages, so time prices more fully capture the benefits of valuable new knowledge and the growth in human capital. Time prices make it easier to see the whole picture.

Second, time prices transcend complications associated with trying to convert current or nominal prices to constant or real prices. Time prices avoid the subjective and disputed adjustments of the Consumer Price Index. They use the nominal price and the nominal hourly income at each point in time, so adjusting for inflation is not necessary.

Third, time prices can be calculated on any product with any currency at any time and any place.

Fourth, time is an objective and universal constant. As economist George Gilder noted, the International System of Units has established seven key metrics, six of which are bounded in one way or another by the passage of time (that is, the equations that specify the unit of measurement use time as a factor). As the only irreversible element in the universe, time is the ultimate frame of reference for all measured values. Science uses time to measure, and so should economics.

> **Innovation lowers prices and increases wages, so time prices more fully capture the benefits of valuable new knowledge and the growth in human capital.**

Fifth, time cannot be inflated or counterfeited. It is fixed and continuous. Everyone has perfect time equality with 24 hours in a day. No matter how much money we have, we can't buy time. If we could, the rich would never die.

Sixth, because we have perfect equality of time with exactly 24 hours in a day, we should compare not income inequality, but what people get to do with their time. If you measure differences in what people do with their time instead of income inequality, you get an entirely different picture of our standard of living. It's not how much income you earn, but what you get to do with your time, that really counts. Time freedom is what we should be measuring.

These six reasons make using time prices superior to using money prices for measuring resource abundance. Time prices are elegant, intuitive, and simple. They are the true prices we pay for the things we buy in life.

THE REASON WE ARE SO RICH IS THAT THERE ARE SO MANY OF US

Many products have high fixed costs and low marginal costs. It costs a lot to develop the product, but then it is cheap to make copies. Take drugs and software, for example.

Drugs. If it costs $1 billion to develop a new drug (as the *Journal of the American Medical Association* has estimated), but each copy of the new pill costs only $1, how much should you sell it for? The answer depends on the size of the market. If the market were 1,000 people, your costs would be $1,000,001,000. You would have to sell each pill for $1,000,001 to break even. If your market were one million people, the breakeven price would drop to $1,001. Go to one billion people and the price per pill drops to $2. This market principle is why new drugs are typically developed for illnesses that lots of people have. The fixed costs must be spread across the market. This is pretty amazing when you think about it. For $2, you get a pill that costs $1 billion to develop, if one billion other people have the same ailment.

> The bigger the population and the more we specialize, the more variety and lower costs we enjoy from one another.

Software. Software is typically all fixed cost and zero marginal cost. Apple has 1.8 million apps and games in its app store. One popular app on the Apple iPhone platform is TouchRetouch, a program that removes unwanted items from images. The German company ADVA Soft GmbH developed the program. Apple charges 30 percent, and plans start at $1.99 per week, so ADVA gets $1.39 for each copy sold at that price. Buying and downloading the app takes less than one minute. Putting your app on the iPhone App Store gives you access to more than one billion active iPhone users. Say it costs ADVA $200,000 to develop its app. ADVA would have to sell 143,884 copies just to break even. After that, it's all profit. If ADVA could sell 300,000 copies, its profit would be $217,000; if sales go up to one million copies, the profit would be $1.19 million.

Adam Smith understood this principle back in 1776. If you want to get rich, have lots of people you can sell to. Large markets also allow people to develop their skills and specialize in such things as drug and software development. The bigger the population and the more we specialize, the more variety and lower costs we enjoy from one another.

REFRIGERATORS

In 1956, you could buy a Frigidaire refrigerator for $469.95. Back then, blue-collar compensation (wages and benefits) was about $2.16 per hour, making the time price about 217.57 hours. In 2022, you could pick one up at Home Depot for $549.00. In 2022, hourly compensation for blue-collar workers had increased to $34.76 per hour, so the time price fell by 93 percent to 15.79 hours. You got 13.78 refrigerators in 2022 for the time price of one in 1956.

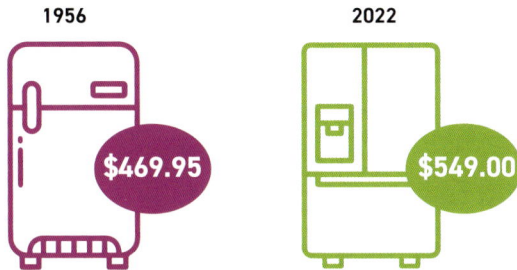

1956 $469.95

2022 $549.00

REFRIGERATORS

	1956	2022	Change	Percentage change
Price	$469.95	$549.00	$79.05	17%
Hourly compensation	$2.16	$34.76	$32.60	1,509%
Time price in hours	217.57	15.79	−201.78	−93%
Personal resource multiplier	1	13.78	12.78	1,278%

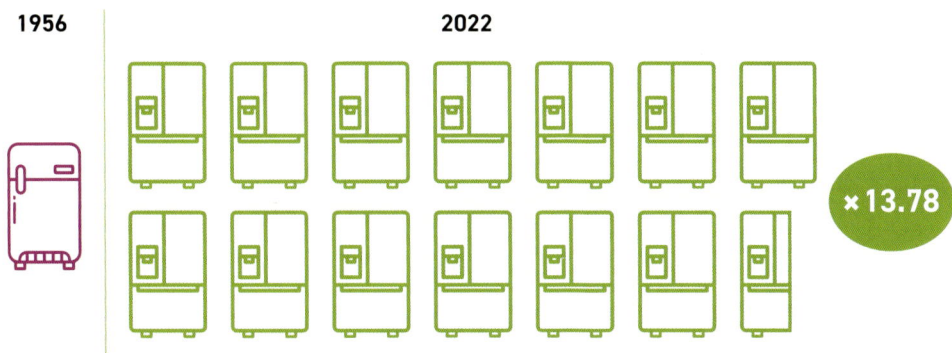

1956

2022

×13.78

AIR CONDITIONING

Air conditioning was invented in 1902 by Willis Carrier in Brooklyn, New York. Carrier invented the unit for a local printing business, which was having problems caused by the hot and humid conditions in its plant. Sweltering Brooklyn summers meant that the paper at the printing plant would often soak up the moisture from the air, which caused the paper to expand and change shape. That ruined the alignment of colors on the printed page, causing financial losses.

Although air conditioning was originally used for industrial purposes, during the postwar economic boom of the 1950s, it surged in popularity and its use expanded to offices, hotels, stores, movie theaters, and private homes. One of the most impressive things about the invention of air conditioning is how quickly it went from a luxury good reserved for only the richest in society to becoming affordable to the masses.

AIR CONDITIONERS

	1952	2022	Change	Percentage change
Price	$350.00	$154.00	−$196.00	−56.0%
Hourly compensation	$1.83	$34.76	$32.93	1,799%
Time price in hours	191.3	4.4	−186.9	−97.7%
Personal resource multiplier	1	43.48	42.48	4,248%

Compound annual growth rate 5.53%   **Years to double** 12.9

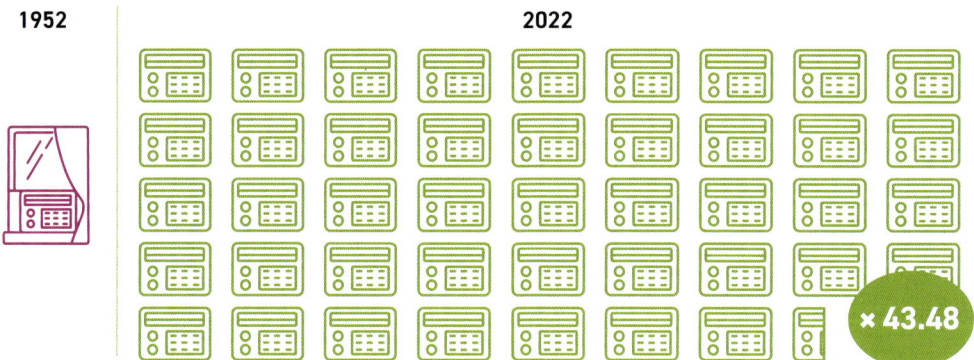

1952

2022

× 43.48

In 1952, the price of a window air-conditioning unit was $350. The website MeasuringWorth.com tells us that a blue-collar worker's hourly wage was $1.83. This wage would put the time price at 191.3 hours. (MeasuringWorth.com, maintained by a team of prominent economists, is widely recognized as one of the most comprehensive and authoritative sources for historical wage data.)

Today, Walmart sells a far more efficient window air-conditioning unit starting around $154, about the same price as in 2022. With the current hourly salary of a blue-collar worker at $34.76, it now takes just 4.4 hours of labor to buy such an air-conditioning unit. That means that the time price of air conditioning has fallen by 97.7 percent since 1952.

Put differently, for the same amount of time that it took to buy one air-conditioning unit in 1952, you can buy 43.17 units today. The abundance of personal air conditioning has been growing at a compound annual rate of 5.53 percent, doubling in abundance every 12.9 years.

> One of the most impressive things about the invention of air conditioning is how quickly it went from a luxury good reserved for only the richest in society to becoming affordable to the masses.

COMPOUND ANNUAL GROWTH RATES

How do you compare the change in abundance between a chocolate bar from 1900, a refrigerator from 1956, and an air conditioner from 1952? Things can grow in different ways. They can grow by a fixed amount, or they can grow by a percentage. When they grow by a percentage, economists call that "compound" growth. To illustrate, consider the following example by comparison:

- If you plant a tree that is 10 inches tall and it grows 2 inches each year, at the end of 10 years it will be 30 inches tall.

10 inches   →   30 inches tall
0 years   10 years

- If you plant that same tree and it grows by 20 percent a year, at the end of the first year it will be 12 inches tall, just as with linear growth. But in the second year, it will grow by 2.4 inches—20 percent of 10 inches plus 20 percent of 2 inches. Each year you get growth from what you started out with *plus* all the growth from previous years. At the end of 10 years, it will be 61.9 inches tall. The 31.9-inch difference is due to the growth on the growth.

10 inches — 62.2 inches tall
0 years 10 years

The rate of growth in the second scenario is called the compound annual growth rate (CAGR).

Year	Linear	Annual growth	Compound	Annual growth
0	10.0		10.0	
1	12.0	2.0	12.0	2.0
2	14.0	2.0	14.4	2.4
3	16.0	2.0	17.3	2.9
4	18.0	2.0	20.8	3.5
5	20.0	2.0	25.0	4.2
6	22.0	2.0	30.0	5.0
7	24.0	2.0	36.0	6.0
8	26.0	2.0	43.2	7.2
9	28.0	2.0	51.8	8.6
10	30.0	2.0	62.2	10.4

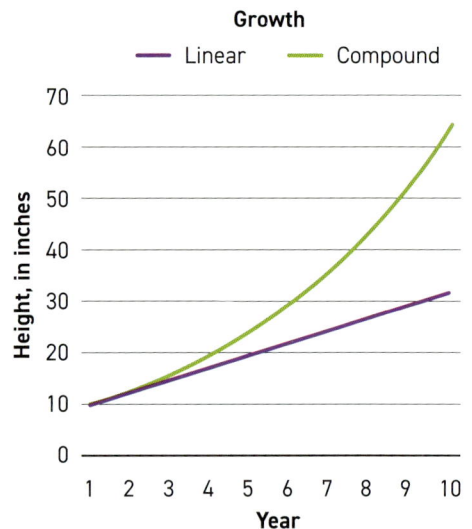

Growth

Linear Compound

Height, in inches

Economists have developed the CAGR to account for total growth and calculate change on an annualized basis. This approach provides a standardized way to make comparisons between any two products independent of their time ranges. It allows you to compare a chocolate bar from 1900, a refrigerator from 1956, and an air conditioner from 1952. You can use a financial calculator or a spreadsheet program like Excel or Google Sheets to get the answer using the RATE function. From this approach you can see which product had the highest compound growth rate.

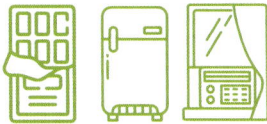

	Start year	End year	Years	End-year personal resource multiplier	Compound annual growth rate
Chocolate bars	1900	2022	122	7	1.56%
Refrigerators	1956	2022	66	13.78	4.05%
Air conditioners	1952	2022	70	43.48	5.53%
Average					**3.71%**

YEARS TO DOUBLE

Another important question is "How long does it take for something to double in size?"

If the growth rate is linear, that question is pretty easy to answer. But if the growth is compounding, it is a bit more difficult. We can use logarithms, but that's not fun. You can use a financial calculator or a spreadsheet program to get the answer using the Number of Periods, or NPER function, which is used in finance and economics to calculate how long it takes for values to grow.

	Compound annual growth rate	Years to double
Chocolate bars	1.56%	44.87
Refrigerators	4.05%	17.28
Air conditioners	5.53%	12.66%
Average	**3.71%**	**25.03**

But we can get an estimate by using a shortcut called the "Rule of 70s." The rule is based on the simple equation of 70 divided by the CAGR. If we know the CAGRs, we can calculate the years to double for chocolate bars, refrigerators, and air conditioners, as shown in the table above.

Now let's look at some more products using time prices and see how much abundance has changed along with the CAGRs and years to double.

BREAKFAST

The book *Superabundance* compared the prices of 12 breakfast items in 1919 to prices in 2019. The items included bacon, bread, butter, coffee, cornflakes, Cream of Wheat, eggs, ham, milk, oranges, rolled oats, and sugar. The 1919 prices were provided by the US Bureau of Labor Statistics (BLS), and the 2019 prices were compiled at Walmart.

Shoppers in 1919 would spend about $4.18 to buy all 12 of these items. With blue-collar worker compensation at $0.43 per hour, it would take them about 9.72 hours of work to stock up their breakfast pantry and icebox. By 2019, the breakfast basket bill had increased to $32.96,

Commodity	1919 BLS nominal price	2019 Walmart nominal price	Nominal price change	Percentage change in nominal price
Bacon sliced, lb.	$0.53	$3.68	$3.15	594.3%
Bread, lb., baked weight	$0.10	$1.28	$1.18	1,180.0%
Butter, lb.	$0.67	$3.04	$2.37	353.7%
Coffee, lb.	$0.43	$4.00	$3.57	830.2%
Cornflakes, 8 oz. pkg.	$0.14	$0.40	$0.26	185.7%
Cream of Wheat, 28 oz. pkg.	$0.25	$3.48	$3.23	1,292.0%
Eggs, dozen	$0.61	$1.28	$0.67	109.8%
Ham, sliced, lb.	$0.57	$3.00	$2.43	426.3%
Milk, fresh, quart	$0.15	$0.96	$0.85	540.0%
Oranges, dozen	$0.53	$10.56	$10.03	1,892.5%
Rolled oats, lb.	$0.08	$0.96	$0.91	1,137.5%
Sugar, granulated, lb.	$0.11	$0.32	$0.21	190.9%
Summary	**$4.17**	**$32.96**	**$28.86**	**727.8%**

but hourly compensation increased to $32.36, so it took just over one hour to buy the same basket of 12 items.

Compared with workers in 1919, workers in 2019 had about 8.7 additional free hours to do something else besides working to pay for breakfast. They could enjoy more leisure, learn a new skill, earn money to buy something else, or take a nap. In this sense, innovation gives us all more time freedom.

Time prices decreased by an average of 93 percent. For the time required to buy one basket of these breakfast items in 1919, you get 9.54 baskets in 2019. This is an 854 percent increase in personal breakfast abundance, which has been increasing at a compound annual rate of about 2.28 percent per year, doubling every 31 years.

1919 time price at $0.43 per hour	2019 time price at $32.36 per hour	1919–2019 percentage change in time price	1919–2019 average personal resource abundance multiplier	1919–2019 average percentage change in personal resource abundance
1.23	0.11	−91.1%	11.18	1,018%
0.24	0.04	−83.3%	6.00	500%
1.56	0.09	−94.2%	17.33	1,634%
1.00	0.12	−88.0%	8.33	733%
0.33	0.01	−97.0%	33.00	3,200%
0.58	0.11	−81.0%	5.27	427%
1.43	0.04	−97.2%	35.75	3,475%
1.32	0.09	−93.2%	14.67	1,367%
0.36	0.03	−91.7%	12.00	1,100%
1.23	0.33	−73.2%	3.73	273%
0.18	0.03	−83.3%	6.00	500%
0.26	0.01	−96.2%	26.00	2,500%
9.72	**1.01**	**−89.1%**	**14.94**	**1,394%**

MILEAGE

Oldsmobile Cutlass — 20 mpg

Honda CR-V — 31 mpg

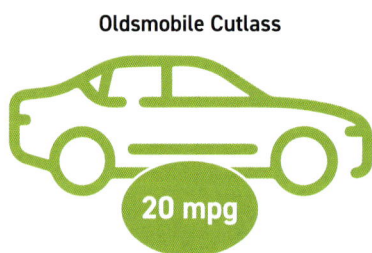

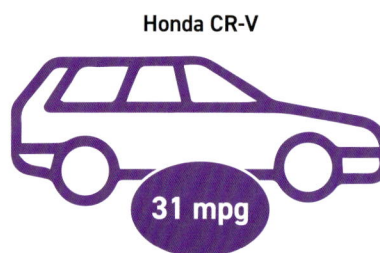

The top-selling car in 1980 was the Oldsmobile Cutlass. Gas mileage on this vehicle averaged 20 miles per gallon (17 city/23 highway). By 2021, the Honda CR-V had claimed the title. The CR-V reported mileage at 31 miles per gallon (28 city/34 highway). That gas mileage represents an increase of 55 percent over the 41-year period. Mileage has been increasing at a compound rate of about 1 percent a year.

Back in 1980, gasoline was selling for $1.19 per gallon and blue-collar hourly compensation (wages and benefits) was $9.12 per hour. Those rates indicate a time price of about 7.83 minutes per gallon. In 2022, gasoline was selling for about $4.06 per gallon and blue-collar hourly compensation was up to $34.76 per hour, indicating a time price of about 7 minutes per gallon. Although the nominal price of a gallon of gasoline has increased by 241 percent, the time price has dropped by 10 percent.

But how much does it cost to travel one mile? That depends on the time price of gasoline and the car's mileage. In 1980 at 20 miles per gallon, the time price per mile on the Cutlass would be about 23.5 seconds. By 2022, with the CR-V getting 31 miles per gallon, the time price per mile would be about 13.6 seconds. The time price per mile has decreased by 42 percent.

Start year	Gallon of gasoline nominal price	Nominal blue-collar hourly compensation	Gallon of gasoline time price in minutes	Miles per gallon (MPG)	Time price per mile in seconds	Miles per minute of time	Car price	Car time price
1980	$1.19	$9.12	7.83	20.00	23.49	2.55	$6,735	738
2022	$4.06	$34.76	7.01	31.00	13.56	4.42	$28,334	815
Percent change	241%	281%	–10%	55%	–42%	73%	321%	10%

You can look at mileage from the perspective of how many miles you get per minute of time. The 1980 Cutlass gave you 2.55 miles per minute of your time, while the 2022 CR-V gives you 4.42 miles. Gas mileage abundance from your time perspective has *increased* by 42 percent.

There are other differences to consider. J.D. Power reported the price of a new Cutlass in 1980 at $6,735. At $9.12 per hour, it would have taken a blue-collar worker 738 hours to own this new car. The 2022 CR-V retailed for about $28,334 new. At $34.76 per hour, it would take the worker 815 hours to buy one. So, although the time price of the top-selling car has increased by 10 percent, the mileage, safety, reliability, and comfort have all increased by much more.

The increase in safety has been especially spectacular. Traffic deaths per vehicle mile have fallen 57 percent since 1980.

BURRITOS

College students across America love bean burritos. They provide about 280 calories of energy, 33 grams of carbohydrates, and 7 grams of protein. But they didn't really become popular until the innovation of the microwave oven.

The microwave was invented accidentally in 1945 by Percy Spencer, a self-taught engineer. While testing a new vacuum tube called a magnetron, he discovered that a chocolate bar in his pocket had melted from the heat. He then tried popcorn. The results were beautiful. He built a metal box with an opening at one end to trap the high-density magnetic energy field inside, allowing the energy to bounce around and quickly heat up the food. The first microwave oven was born. Eleven years later, in 1956, Duane R. Roberts invented the frozen burrito. We now had the two key elements for an innovation in college dorm cuisine.

In 1979, microwaves were selling at Sears for $399.85. Unskilled workers back then were earning about $3.69 per hour, which made the time price 108.4 hours. But in 2022, unskilled workers earned about $15.72 per hour, and a basic microwave at Walmart sold for around $55, about the same as today. That would put the time price at about 3.5 hours. The time price fell by 96.8 percent. Microwave innovation has given us an extra 103.7 hours today compared with 1979. For the time it took Grandpa to earn the money to buy his microwave 43 years ago, you can get more than 23 microwaves today. Microwave abundance has been growing at a 7.57 percent compound annual rate, doubling in abundance every 9.5 years. Microwaves are an example of adding knowledge to energy and the material atoms that make up the things around us to make them more valuable and more abundant.

With a microwave, the time to heat up a burrito fell 95.5 percent from 28 minutes to about 2 minutes. Every time you want a tasty burrito, microwaves stand ready to

Microwaves are an example of adding knowledge to energy and the material atoms that make up the things around us to make them more valuable and more abundant.

give you an extra 26 minutes and 45 seconds. You're given this time whether you are a highly paid engineer or a struggling student. Innovation reduces time without respect to your income level.

Microwaves also use about one-third the energy of a conventional oven. At $0.20 per kilowatt hour, the use of a conventional oven to heat up a burrito will cost about $0.28 versus less than half a penny (0.41 cents) for a microwave. The energy cost to warm up that quick bite has fallen 98.5 percent. Knowledge gives us more time freedom, one of our most valuable resources.

TELEVISION

The first successful transmission of an all-electronic television signal occurred on September 7, 1927, in the laboratory of Philo T. Farnsworth in San Francisco. The idea came to him at age 14 when he was plowing fields with horses on an Idaho farm. At age 21, Farnsworth secured a $25,000 bank loan to pursue his vision, and the rest is history. As TV industry veteran Phil Savenick notes on his History of Television website:

> Born in a log cabin in Utah in 1906, Philo Taylor Farnsworth grew up in the Old West. His father drove a stagecoach and their farm had no electricity. He had no telephone, no computer, not even lights at night. After seeing a locomotive at the age of six, he decided he wanted to become an inventor. A summer job near Rigby, Idaho, provided the fertile soil for his "big idea." The barn contained a stash of science fiction magazines that promised a future with flying cars, picture phones, and mechanical television. By learning to repair the farm's broken Delco generator, he began his lifelong fascination with electrons.

Technology writer Brian Roemmele notes that from 1939 to 1941 about 7,000 television sets were sold in the United States. Television broadcasts were limited to a few large cities such as New York and Los Angeles. This new technology was out of reach for most Americans because sets ranged from $200 to $600.

In 1940, an unskilled worker earned about $0.33 per hour. This wage would put the time price of a $400 TV at 1,212 hours. Today, you can buy a 43-inch ultra-high-definition TV for $199.95 at Walmart. In 2022, unskilled workers earned about $15.72 per hour, which put the time price at just 12.7 hours.

> **Without the innovation of TV, there would be no internet or mobile phones. It is a foundational technology for the age of knowledge discovery.**

It is estimated that 96 percent of American homes have at least one TV. Statista estimates that, worldwide, 1.74 billion of the 2.15 billion households, or 81 percent of all households, have at least one TV. In addition, an estimated 200 million units are sold each year. Without the innovation of TV, there would be no internet or mobile phones. It is a foundational technology for the age of knowledge discovery.

America had the types of capital needed for this innovation: the idea, the freedom, the financial resources, the technical talent, and the market. Thank you, Mr. Farnsworth, for your imagination and dedication to making your vision a reality.

LISTENING TO MUSIC

The first phonograph record was developed by Thomas Edison in 1877. The first playable records were made from paper pressed between two pieces of tin foil. On March 15, 1949, RCA Victor became the first label to roll out 45 RPM vinyl records. They were smaller and held less music than the popular 78s and were printed in different colors from deep red to dark blue. As David Browne noted in a 2019 *Rolling Stone* article, "Teenagers of the Fifties took to the portable, less-expensive format; one ad at the time priced the records at 65 cents each. One of rock's most cataclysmic early hits, Bill Haley and the Comets' 'Rock Around the Clock,' sold 3 million singles in 1955."

> **Music abundance is growing more than 10 times faster than population. Abundance allows us the time freedom to create more abundance.**

Unskilled workers in 1955 earned about $0.97 per hour. That would put the time price of a song at 40 minutes. Apple introduced the iTunes Store on April 28, 2003, and sold individual songs for $0.99. By this time, unskilled wages had increased to $9.25 per hour. The time price of a song had dropped 84 percent to 6.42 minutes. Listeners in 2003 got six songs for the price of one in 1955.

In June 2015, Apple launched its Apple Music streaming service. In 2022, a student could get access to 100 million songs for $5.99 a month. Unskilled workers earned about $15.72 per hour, so the time price was about 23 minutes. The time price per song is about one-ninth of a second. For the time it took our grandparents to earn the money to buy one song back in 1955, we got a nearly unlimited music library in 2022. And, of course, Apple Music is far from the only game in town, thanks to strong competition from services like Spotify and Pandora.

This expansion happened while the global population grew by 5.2 billion, or 185 percent, from 2.8 billion to 8 billion. That means that the world's population grew at a 1.58 percent compound annual growth rate during that time. Music abundance is growing more than 10 times faster than population. Abundance allows us the time freedom to create more abundance.

All the products we enjoy around us today are the culmination of billions and billions of little bits of knowledge that human beings have discovered and then shared with the rest of us in free markets. Create a song and share it with the planet. We can lift one another and make people's lives better.

SHIPPING

Yuval Noah Harari notes in a 2021 *Financial Times* article that in 1582, the English merchant fleet had a total carrying capacity of 68,000 tons and required about 16,000 sailors. The container ship *Ever Alot*, christened in 2022, can carry some 236,228 tons while requiring a crew of only 22. One ship today carries 3.47 times more than the whole English fleet did 440 years ago. The English fleet required one sailor for every 4.25 tons, while the *Ever Alot* ships 10,738 tons per sailor. The *Ever Alot* measures 1,312 feet by 203 feet and holds up to 24,004 20-foot equivalent units. If these containers were placed end to end, they would stretch for almost 91 miles.

Malcom McLean, the inventor of the intermodal shipping container, was perhaps the greatest innovator in shipping. In 1956, hand-loading cargo onto a ship in a US port cost $5.86 per ton. By 2006, shipping containers, which can be unloaded from ships quickly onto trucks, and vice versa, had reduced that price to just $0.16 per ton. Converting these nominal prices to time prices using blue-collar hourly compensation (wages and benefits) data from MeasuringWorth.com indicates a reduction of 99.8 percent in loading costs. For the time required to earn the money to pay to load one ton in 1956, you can get 440 tons loaded today. Loading has become 43,900 percent more abundant.

Things can be shipped five ways: roads, rail, sea, air, and pipelines. In his book *Business Logistics: Supply Chain Management*, Professor Ronald Ballou estimated the following rates per ton-mile: For the cost of shipping one ton by air, you can ship more than 80 tons by ship. Shipping by air from Shanghai to Los Angeles takes about 12 hours, while container ships take 13 days. Ships take 26 times longer but are 98.75 percent cheaper.

That ability to move things across vast distances endows the atoms that make up those things with value, which is related to their use. We don't want some atoms to move—like, for example, those that hold up a building. If the atoms that make up a building move, they lose their value—and the building falls down. But other atoms, like those that make up merchandise, can lose their value if they *aren't* moving. Quickly being able to move them to higher-valued locations becomes very important. Containerization has added tremendous value to atoms because it is now much cheaper and faster to move them. Although we have the

> As long as human beings are free to innovate by discovering and creating things and sharing valuable new knowledge, our resources have no limit, because knowledge has no limit.

same number of atoms on our planet today as we did in 1582, our knowledge has grown tremendously. It is knowledge that makes atoms valuable. Knowledge transforms atoms into resources. As long as human beings are free to innovate by discovering and creating things and sharing valuable new knowledge, our resources have no limit, because knowledge has no limit. Malcom McLean, who enjoyed the freedom to innovate and share his creativity in a free market, helped increase the world's wealth in ways no one previously imagined.

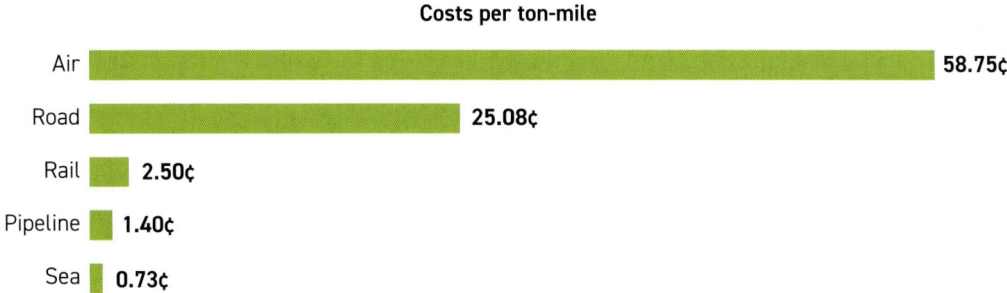

Costs per ton-mile

Air	58.75¢
Road	25.08¢
Rail	2.50¢
Pipeline	1.40¢
Sea	0.73¢

PONIES TO PHOTONS

Before April 3, 1860, when the Pony Express ran its first route, it took 25 days to send a message 1,900 miles from St. Joseph, Missouri, to Sacramento, California. On that day, the innovative Pony Express cut delivery times to 10 days and reigned for 18 months as the fastest way to deliver information across the United States. Riders traveled 75 to 100 miles, switching horses every 10 to 15 miles.

In its early days, the service cost $5 for every half ounce of mail. Blue-collar hourly compensation (wages and benefits) in 1861 was $0.08 per hour, so it took 62.5 hours of work to pay for a half-ounce letter. Blue-collar workers earn around $35 per hour today, so the cost of sending a letter would be equivalent to $2,187 today. The Pony Express later reduced the price to just $1, which is about $437.50 today.

Ponies to Electrons

Western Union started building the first transcontinental telegraph on July 4, 1861. It was completed 112 days later on October 24, 1861. Two days later, the Pony Express was discontinued.

Pony Express horses traveled about 10 miles per hour. Electrons on a telegraph line travel 670,616,629 miles per hour, almost as fast as the speed of light.

With the telegraph, electrons replaced horses as the fastest way to send a message. A human operator using a telegraph could send about five bits per second. Communication speed made steady progress as telegraphs evolved into telephones and teletype machines.

Telephones allowed us to talk with one another in real time, but human beings process only about 39 bits of speech per second. Copper wires can handle that level of communication. But talking to each other is just a small fraction of the communication we do today. To move massive amounts of information, such as text, images, and sound, we needed to go from analog to digital. We needed to convert these things to bits. Electrons can do bits, but photons are much better at it.

Electrons to Photons

To move more bits at a faster rate, we had to move beyond sending electrons through copper wire to a way to send photons, or light. This feat was accomplished with the innovation of fiber-optic cables using highly pure glass. Almost all communication today travels through a fiber-optic cable at some stage.

How fast are fiber optics and photons? Michael Irving reported in a 2022 *New Atlas* article that engineers in Denmark and Sweden using an optical chip have been able to send 1.84 petabits per second down a 4.9-mile fiber-optic cable. A peta is 10 raised to the power of 15, or a thousand trillion. A petabit is 1,000,000,000,000,000 (one quadrillion) bits. That is almost twice the global internet traffic per second. The researchers claim that it could eventually reach speeds of up to 100 petabits per second, or 54 times faster. This new speed record is more than 80 percent faster than the previous record set just five months earlier. In mid-2020, the speed record was 44 terabits per second. Given that 1.84 petabits is 1,840 terabits, this new chip is 42 times faster than the fastest chip was just two years earlier.

Much as Moore's Law predicted that the number of transistors on a computer microchip would double every two years, the human capacity for transmitting information is growing at an exponential rate. The new chip can send 1.5 million years of human speech in one second.

> **Thanks to the millions of dedicated engineers and entrepreneurs and the freedom to innovate, our world is about to experience astonishing creativity.**

Our ability to share bits is truly wonderful. With eight billion human beings on the planet now and around seven billion smartphones with inexpensive access to the world's knowledge, we have never had a time when our ability to learn and communicate has been better. Thanks to the millions of dedicated engineers and entrepreneurs and the freedom to innovate, our world is about to experience astonishing creativity.

COUNTERTOP KITCHEN APPLIANCES

Has innovation improved kitchen appliances? To answer this question, my *Superabundance* coauthor and I went back to the 1980 fall/winter Sears catalog and looked at the prices of five countertop kitchen appliances—a coffeemaker, toaster, blender, mixer, and food processor. The total cost to buy all these items was $219.94. In 1980, unskilled workers earned about $4.06 per hour, so it took 54.17 hours of work to equip your kitchen with these modern appliances.

We then searched Walmart's website to find similar items. The nominal prices in 2020 for the five items had dropped by 57.32 percent to $93.87. However, nominal unskilled wages had increased by 253.7 percent to $14.36 per hour, so it took only 6.54 hours of work to buy these five appliances in 2020. The time price had fallen by 87.9 percent. Kitchen appliance abundance increased by an average of 731.4 percent, from 254 percent for blenders to 2,023 percent for food processors.

For the time required to buy a set of these appliances for one house in 1980, you could furnish 8.29 houses in 2020. Abundance in the kitchen has been increasing at a compound annual rate of about 5.43 percent a year. At this rate, abundance doubles every 13 years. As you prepare your dinner this evening, take a moment and thank the many kitchen appliance innovators who have given every home an extra 47.63 hours of life to enjoy.

	1980 price (Sears)	1980 time price at $4.06 per hour	2020 price (Walmart)	2020 time price at $14.36 per hour	Percentage change in time price	Increase in abundance
Coffeemaker	$31.99	7.88 hrs.	$13.90	0.97 hrs.	−87.7%	+712%
Toaster	$19.99	4.92 hrs.	$14.96	1.04 hrs.	−78.9%	+373%
Blender	$19.99	4.92 hrs.	$19.96	1.39 hrs.	−71.8%	+254%
Hand mixer	$10.99	2.71 hrs.	$9.88	0.69 hrs.	−74.5%	+293%
Food processor	$119.99	29.55 hrs.	$19.99	1.39 hrs.	−95.3%	+2,026%
Average	**$40.59**	**10 hrs.**	**$15.74**	**1.01 hrs.**	**−81.6%**	**+731.4%**

WATER

How much water is there in the world for us to drink? Depends on how you look at it. "Water, water, every where, Nor any drop to drink," lamented Coleridge's ancient mariner. Yet these days, desalination is incredibly cheap.

According to the website Filtration and Separation, in 2012, the cost to desalinate was $0.75 per cubic meter. In 2012, US unskilled labor hourly wages were $10.97. In 2022, they had increased to $15.72, and the cost to desalinate had decreased to $0.41 per cubic meter. That would put the time price in 2012 at 4.14 minutes and in 2022 at 1.56 minutes. Today, we're getting 165 percent more gallons of clean water for the same time it took in 2012. Water abundance from desalination is growing at a 10.22 percent compound annual rate, doubling in abundance every seven years. This change happened at the same time we added 860 million people to the planet. Population was growing at a 1.14 percent annual rate, while desalination grew almost nine times faster.

WATER	2012	2022	Change	Percentage change
Price	$0.75	$0.41	−$0.34	−45%
Hourly compensation	$10.97	$15.72	$4.75	43%
Time price in minutes	4.14	1.56	−2.58	−62%
Personal resource multiplier	1	2.65	1.65	165%

CHAPTER 2

MEASURING ABUNDANCE AT THE POPULATION LEVEL

In the previous chapter we measured abundance at the personal or individual level. In this chapter we will learn how to measure abundance at the population or global level. To determine abundance at the population level, we multiply personal resource abundance by the size of the population. We make this calculation at two points in time and then compare the difference to see what has happened to resource abundance at the global level.

SANDWICH ABUNDANCE

Let's imagine that in the year 2002 it cost you one hour to earn the money to buy a sandwich. Fast-forward to 2022. In this scenario, two things have changed. First, let's say that, thanks to innovation and productivity, the time price has decreased by 75 percent to only 15 minutes. You now can buy the same sandwich in one-fourth of the time it took you 20 years ago. Your personal sandwich abundance has increased by 300 percent. Let's say that the second thing that changed is that your household size has doubled. There are now two people in your household. The second person also enjoys the same sandwich abundance as you, so your household sandwich abundance has increased from one in 2002 to eight in 2022. This rise would be a 700 percent increase in sandwich abundance at the household population level.

SANDWICHES	2002	2022	Change	Percentage change
Personal abundance	1	4	3	300%
× Population	1	2	1	100%
= Population abundance	1	8	7	700%

We can chart this analysis with personal sandwich abundance on the vertical axis and the population size on the horizontal axis:

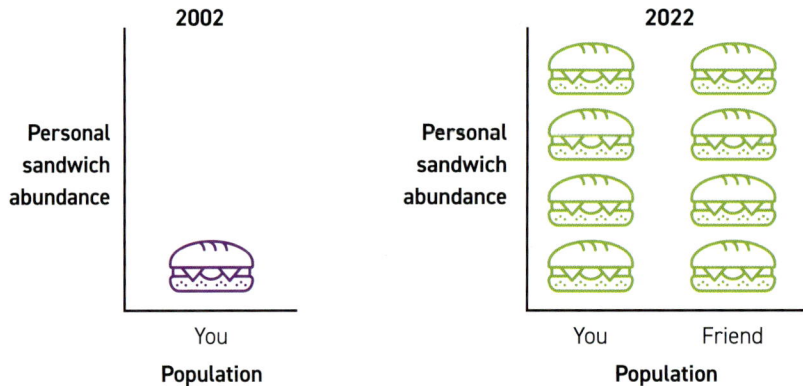

You can make a simple chart to illustrate abundance at both the personal and population level for any product or service. We call this illustration a start-year/end-year box chart. Plot personal resource abundance on the vertical axis and population on the horizontal axis. Select a start-year point and set both dimensions to a value of one. That step will give you a one-by-one box equal to one. Then plot the end-year point of the analysis and compare the two.

Let's chart the sandwich abundance example. If the time price of sandwiches decreases by 75 percent, it means you can now buy the same sandwich in one-quarter of the time it used to take you 20 years ago. Personal resource abundance has gone from one to four on the vertical axis, increasing by 300 percent. Because population doubled, the horizontal axis would grow 100 percent from a value of one to a value of two. The end-year box would now measure four by two, or eight. Now place the start-year box over the end-year box. See the difference? Global abundance has increased from one to eight, or 700 percent. These start-year/end-year box charts make it easy to visualize the growth in abundance in the two dimensions of personal abundance and population.

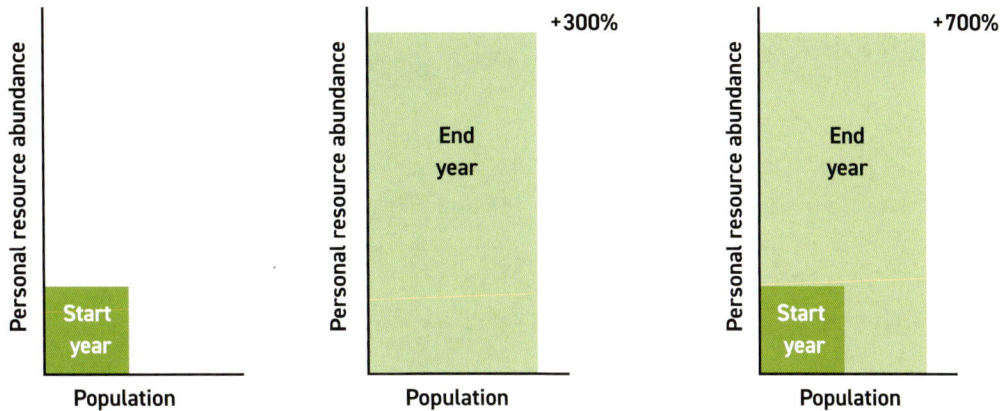

Resource and Population Elasticities

What is the relationship between population and resources? We can quantify and measure his relationship with a concept economists call "elasticity." Elasticity is the ratio of the percentage change in one variable divided by the percentage change in another variable.

For example, if personal sandwich abundance increases by 300 percent while population increases by 100 percent, the ratio would be 300 divided by 100, indicating a value of 3. This ratio suggests that every 1 percent increase in population corresponded with a 3 percent increase in personal sandwich abundance.

We can also look at the relationship between population and resource abundance at the population level. In our example, sandwich abundance at the population level increased by 700 percent as population increased by 100 percent, indicating that every 1 percent increase in population corresponded to a 7 percent increase in population-level sandwich abundance.

Elasticity helps us quantify and measure the relationship between resources and population and begin to see patterns that help us make predictions.

Let's go back and look at a few of our personal resource abundance examples and extend the analysis to the population level.

> **Elasticity helps us quantify and measure the relationship between resources and population.**

CHOCOLATE BARS

For the time required to earn the money to buy one chocolate bar in 1900, you would get 6.62 in 2022. Personal chocolate bar abundance has increased 562 percent. From 1900 to 2022, the US population increased 394 percent from 68 million to 336 million. This growth would indicate that US population-level chocolate bar abundance increased by 3,170 percent. US chocolate bar abundance at the population level grew at a 2.9 percent compound annual growth rate, doubling abundance every 24.25 years. For every 1 percent increase in US population, the population-level chocolate bar abundance increased by 8.04 percent.

CHOCOLATE BARS

	1900	2022	Change	Percentage change
Resource multiplier	1	6.62	5.62	562%
US population in millions	68	336	268	394%
Population resource multiplier	68	2,224	2,156	3,170%
Index to 1900 = 1	1.00	32.70	31.70	3,170%

Chocolate Bar Abundance
1900–2022

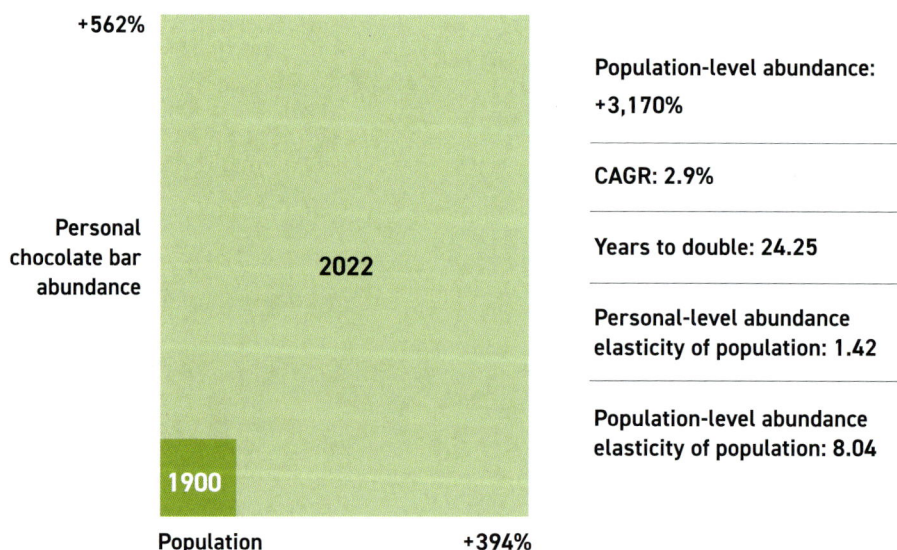

+562%

Personal chocolate bar abundance

2022

1900

Population   **+394%**

Population-level abundance: **+3,170%**

CAGR: **2.9%**

Years to double: **24.25**

Personal-level abundance elasticity of population: **1.42**

Population-level abundance elasticity of population: **8.04**

REFRIGERATORS

For the time required to earn the money to buy one refrigerator in 1956, you would get 13.78 in 2022. Personal refrigerator abundance has increased more than 1,278 percent. From 1956 to 2022, the US population doubled from 168 million to 336 million. This growth would indicate that US population-level refrigerator abundance increased by 2,656 percent. US refrigerator abundance grew at a 5.2 percent compound annual growth rate, doubling abundance every 13.8 years. For every 1 percent increase in the US population, population-level refrigerator abundance increased by 26.56 percent.

REFRIGERATORS

	1956	2022	Change	Percentage change
Resource multiplier	1	13.78	12.78	1,278%
US population in millions	168	336	168	100%
Population resource multiplier	168	4,630.08	4,562.08	2,656%
Index to 1956 = 1	1.00	27.56	26.56	2,656%

Refrigerator Abundance 1956–2022

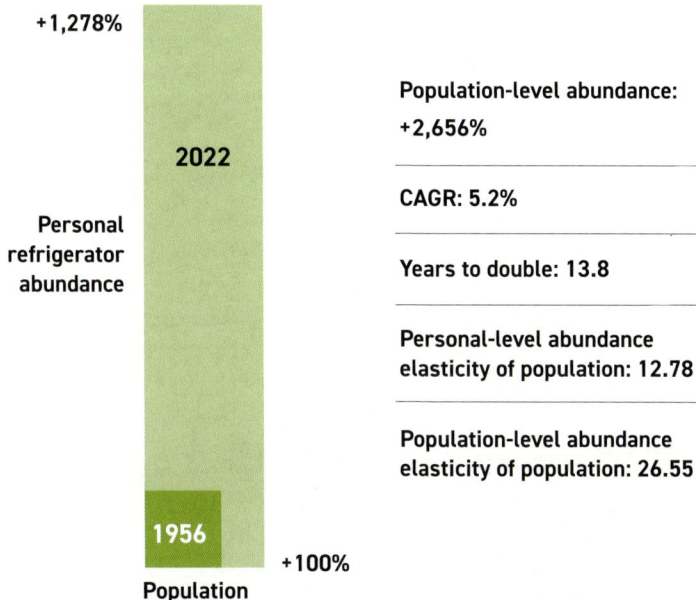

+1,278%

2022

Personal refrigerator abundance

1956

+100%

Population

Population-level abundance: +2,656%

CAGR: 5.2%

Years to double: 13.8

Personal-level abundance elasticity of population: 12.78

Population-level abundance elasticity of population: 26.55

AIR CONDITIONING

For the time required to earn the money to buy one air conditioner in 1952, you would get 43.17 in 2022. Personal air-conditioner abundance has increased 4,217 percent. From 1952 to 2022, the US population more than doubled from 157 million to 336 million. This growth would indicate that US population-level air-conditioner abundance increased by 9,139 percent. US air-conditioner abundance grew at a 6.68 percent compound annual growth rate, doubling abundance every 10.7 years. For every 1 percent increase in US population, population-level air-conditioner abundance increased by 80.16 percent.

AIR CONDITIONERS

	1952	2022	Change	Percentage change
Resource multiplier	1	43.17	42.17	4,217%
US population in millions	157	336	179.00	114%
Population resource multiplier	157	14,505.12	14,348.12	9,139%
Index to 1952 = 1	1.00	92.39	91.39	9,139%

Air-Conditioner Abundance 1952–2022

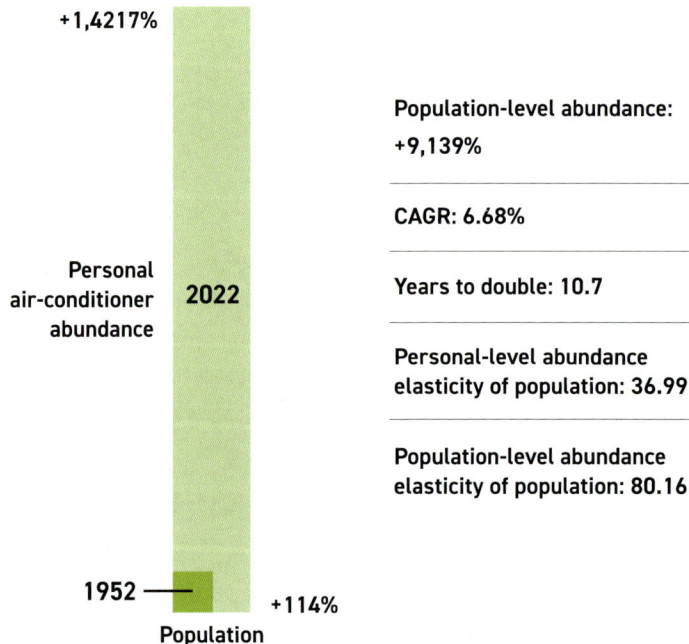

+1,4217%

Personal air-conditioner abundance

2022

1952

+114%

Population

Population-level abundance: +9,139%

CAGR: 6.68%

Years to double: 10.7

Personal-level abundance elasticity of population: 36.99

Population-level abundance elasticity of population: 80.16

ABUNDANCE—LITERALLY—ILLUMINATES THE WORLD

The one commodity that has exceeded them all in increasing abundance appears to be light. Nobel Prize–winning economist William Nordhaus reported that earning the money to buy one hour of light in 1830 required about three hours of labor. Today, with advanced LED technology, one hour of light costs less than one-sixth of a second. For the time it took to earn the money to buy one hour of light in 1830, you get 67,500 hours today. This statistic represents a 6,749,900 percent increase in personal light abundance. Light abundance at the personal level has been increasing 5.97 percent annually, doubling every 12 years.

Over that same period, global population increased 566 percent from 1.2 billion to 8 billion. Every 1 percent increase in population corresponded with an 11,925 percent increase in personal light abundance. The next time you turn on a light switch, please take a moment to appreciate the great work of Thomas Edison and all the free and creative people toiling to bring us out of the darkness. Compared with the abundant light of our world today, our ancestors really did live in the Dark Ages. This chapter applied the time price framework to measure abundance at the population level. Population-level abundance is simply personal abundance multiplied by the population size.

CHAPTER 3

THE SIMON ABUNDANCE INDEX

Economists have long been interested in the bet between Julian Simon and Paul Ehrlich. Several scholars have suggested that Simon was lucky—that if the bet had occurred over a different 10-year period, or if there had been a different set of commodities in the basket, he would have lost to Ehrlich. In 2018, my *Superabundance* coauthor and I decided to reanalyze the bet to see who would win. In an effort to address the two issues about the length of the bet and the number and selection of commodities, we expanded the time period from 10 years to 38 years, from 1980 to 2018. We also increased the number of items in the analysis from 5 to 50. In addition to the five metals, we included a variety of energy, food, materials, and mineral commodities. We were fortunate that the World Bank and the International Monetary Fund track the nominal prices of these commodities on a monthly basis and report their findings.

For each year and each commodity, we converted all the money prices into time prices. The denominator in this analysis is the average global nominal gross domestic product (GDP) per hour worked. The analysis used data from 42 countries and territories, accounting for 85 percent of the global economic output. The earnings data were provided by the World Bank and the Conference Board. From 1980 to 2018, the average global nominal GDP per hour worked rose from $3.24 to $15.88. We found that the average time price of the basic 50 commodities fell by 71.6 percent. If a time price decreases by 71.6 percent, you now get 3.52 units for the time price of 1 unit, or an increase of 252 percent. If you spent the same amount of time working to earn the money in 2018 as you did in 1980 to buy 1 unit, you would have been able to buy 3.52 units in 2018. This change represents a 252 percent increase in your personal abundance.

The following chart illustrates the changes of a selection of 50 commodities from 1980 to 2018. The full list of commodities is available in the book *Superabundance*. The change is illustrated from three perspectives:

- The percentage change in the resource time price
- Personal resource abundance multiplier
- Change in personal resource abundance, compound annual growth rate, and years to double

Commodity	Units	1980 nominal price ($)	2018 nominal price ($)	Percentage change in nominal price (1980–2018)
Bananas	$/lb.	0.34	0.57	67.6
Beef	$/kg	2.76	4.20	52.2
Chicken	$/kg	0.76	2.24	194.7
Cotton	$/kg	2.06	2.01	−2.4
Oranges	$/kg	0.40	0.79	97.5
Plywood	¢/sheet	273.78	494.70	80.7
Rice	$/metric ton	410.74	420.67	2.4
Rubber	$/kg	1.42	1.57	10.6
Sugar	$/kg	0.59	0.41	−30.5
Tea	$/kg	1.66	2.85	71.7

Recall that, to calculate the change in resources at the population level, we also consider changes in population. Over this 38-year period, the global population increased by 71.2 percent. We can now illustrate the changes in both the personal-level resource abundance and population to show the change at the population level.

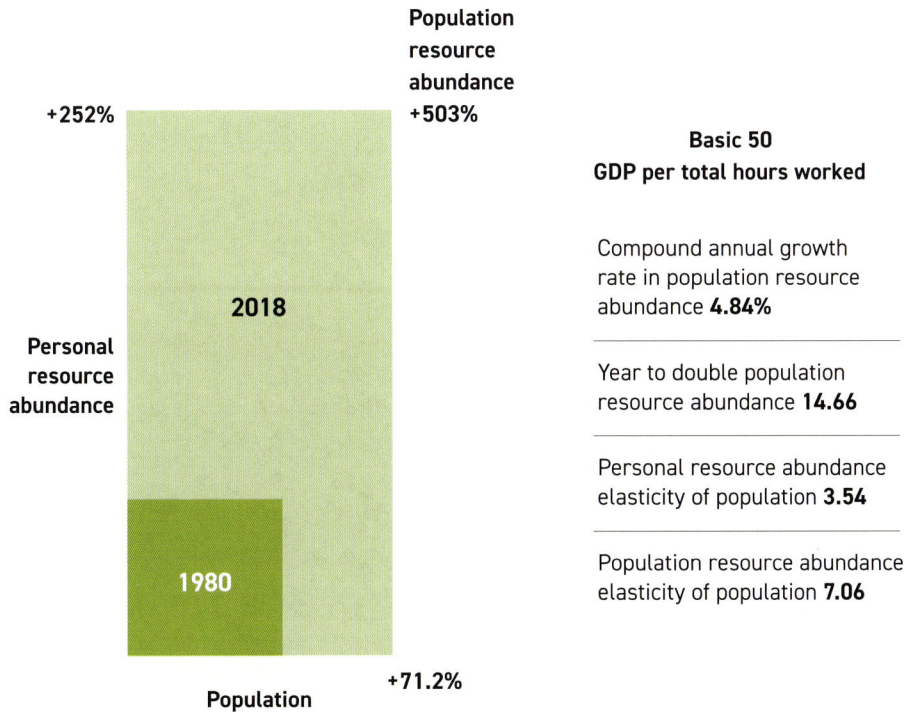

+252%

Population resource abundance +503%

Basic 50 GDP per total hours worked

Compound annual growth rate in population resource abundance **4.84%**

Year to double population resource abundance **14.66**

Personal resource abundance elasticity of population **3.54**

Population resource abundance elasticity of population **7.06**

2018

Personal resource abundance

1980

Population **+71.2%**

Between 1980 and 2018, population resource abundance increased by 503 percent. Population abundance grew at a 4.84 percent compounded annual rate, doubling abundance every 14.66 years. Every 1 percent increase in population corresponded to a 3.54 percent increase in personal resource abundance and a 7.06 percent increase in population resource abundance.

The Simon Abundance Index captures the growth in personal resource abundance and population growth in one value. It uses the average personal resource abundance multiplier from the 50 basic commodities data set and the change in global population to calculate population resource abundance. It has a base year of 1980 and a base value of 100. In 2018, the index reached a level of 602.6. In other words, the earth was 502.6 percent more abundant in 2018 than it was in 1980.

CONCLUSION

Thanos, Paul Ehrlich, and Thomas Malthus all claimed that resources were finite and that if the world's population continued to increase, life would cease to exist. The evidence compellingly rejects their worldview. In fact, as population increases, resources become even more abundant, or "superabundant." Why? Because we are discovering valuable new knowledge faster than we are growing in population.

A Beginner's Guide to Superabundance provides a new way to measure our standard of living using time and a variety of examples. The examples are a small sample of millions of products that reflect the astonishing increase in knowledge we are experiencing. We don't notice this rate of increase for the same reason we don't realize we're moving 550 miles per hour when we take a commercial airline flight. We also don't think about the millions of complex parts and millions of lines of computer code and millions of people involved in making that experience pleasant and safe. We also don't think of the billions of dollars invested in the airline industry to make our flight safe, comfortable, and fast. The overwhelming abundance of evidence gives us great hope that we can discover and create the true wealth of knowledge for ourselves and all those around us.

QUIZ

Here is a short quiz to test your knowledge.

A pizza costs $20 today and you are earning $30 per hour. Twenty years ago, pizzas were $10 and you were earning $8 per hour. Answer the following questions:

1. What is the time price today?

2. What was the time price 20 years ago?

3. How much has the time price decreased?

4. How much has pizza abundance increased?

Extra Credit (Use the RATE function in a spreadsheet program.)

5. What is the compound annual growth rate in pizza abundance?

6. How many years will it take for pizza abundance to double?

ANSWERS

1. 0.667 hour or 40 minutes;
2. 1.25 hours or 75 minutes
3. (40/75) - 1 = -46.7%
4. (75/40) - 1 = +87.5%
5. 3.19%
6. 22 years

ABOUT THE AUTHOR

Gale L. Pooley has taught economics and statistics at Utah Tech University, Brigham Young University–Hawaii, Brigham Young University–Idaho, Boise State University, the College of Idaho, and Alfaisal University in Riyadh, Saudi Arabia. He has held professional designations from the Appraisal Institute, the Royal Institution of Chartered Surveyors, and the CCIM Institute. Pooley has published articles in the *Wall Street Journal*, *Forbes*, *National Review*, HumanProgress.org, the Foundation for Economic Education, the *Utah Bar Journal*, the *Appraisal Journal*, *Quillette*, and *RealClearMarkets*. Pooley is a senior fellow with the Discovery Institute, an adjunct scholar with the Cato Institute, a board member of HumanProgress.org, and a scholar with the Grassroot Institute of Hawaii.

ABOUT CATO INSTITUTE

Founded in 1977, the Cato Institute is a public policy research foundation dedicated to broadening the parameters of policy debate to allow consideration of more options that are consistent with the traditional American principles of limited government, individual liberty, and peace. To that end, the Institute strives to achieve greater involvement of the intelligent, concerned lay public in questions of policy and the proper role of government.

The Institute is named for *Cato's Letters*, libertarian pamphlets that were widely read in the American Colonies in the early 18th century and that played a major role in laying the philosophical foundation for the American Revolution.

Despite the achievement of the nation's Founders, today virtually no aspect of life is free from government encroachment. A pervasive intolerance for individual rights is shown by government's arbitrary intrusions into private economic transactions and its disregard for civil liberties.

To counter that trend, the Cato Institute undertakes an extensive publications program that addresses the complete spectrum of policy issues. Books, monographs, and shorter studies are commissioned to examine the federal budget, Social Security, regulation, military spending, international trade, and myriad other issues.

In order to maintain its independence, the Cato Institute accepts no government funding. Contributions are received from foundations, corporations, and individuals, and other revenue is generated from the sale of publications. The Institute is a nonprofit, tax-exempt, educational foundation under Section 501(c)3 of the Internal Revenue Code.